LAND

SEA

& SKY

Poems to Celebrate the Earth

Selected and illustrated with photographs by

CATHERINE PALADINO

Little, Brown and Company

Boston   Toronto   London

*Grateful acknowledgments to Paul C. Soffron, director and founder of
the North American Wolf Foundation, Inc., in Ipswich, Massachusetts,
for allowing photographs to be taken of his wolves.*

Copyright © 1993 by Catherine Paladino

First Edition

Thanks are given as follows for permission to reprint copyrighted material: **Harry Behn:** "Trees," from *The Little Hill,
Poems and Pictures,* by Harry Behn. Copyright 1949 by Harry Behn. Copyright renewed 1977 by Alice L. Behn. Reprinted by
permission of Marian Reiner. **John Ciardi:** "How to Tell the Top of a Hill," from *The Reason for the Pelican,* by John Ciardi.
J. B. Lippincott Company, 1959. Reprinted by permission of Judith H. Ciardi. **Theodore Clymer:** "My great corn plants,"
from *Four Corners of the Sky: Poems, Chants and Oratory,* selected by Theodore Clymer, illustrated by Marc Brown. Text
copyright © 1975 by Theodore Clymer. Reprinted by permission of Little, Brown and Company. **Emily Dickinson:** "I'll
tell you how the sun rose," from *The Poems of Emily Dickinson,* Thomas H. Johnson, ed. Cambridge, Mass.: The Belknap
Press of Harvard University Press. Copyright 1951, © 1955, 1979, 1983 by the President and Fellows of Harvard College.
Reprinted by permission of the publishers and the Trustees of Amherst College. **Aileen Fisher:** "Looking Around," from
Out in the Dark and Daylight. Text copyright © 1980 by Aileen Fisher. Reprinted by permission of HarperCollins Publishers.
"Snowstorm," from *In the Woods, In the Meadow, In the Sky,* by Aileen Fisher. Charles Scribner's Sons, 1965. Reprinted by
permission of Aileen Fisher. **Rachel Field:** "The Little Rose Tree," from *Poems,* by Rachel Field. New York: Macmillan,
1957. Reprinted by permission of Macmillan Publishing Company. **Paul Fleischman:** "The Passenger Pigeon," from *I Am
Phoenix: Poems for Two Voices,* by Paul Fleischman. Text copyright © 1985 by Paul Fleischman. Reprinted by permission of
HarperCollins Publishers. **Mary Ann Hoberman:** "Whale," from *The Raucous Auk,* Viking, 1973. Reprinted by permission
of Gina Maccoby Literary Agency. Copyright © 1973 by Mary Ann Hoberman. **Felice Holman:** "Who Am I?" from *At the Top of
My Voice and Other Poems,* Charles Scribner's Sons. Copyright © 1970. Reprinted by permission of Felice Holman. **Langston
Hughes:** "April Rain Song," from *The Dream Keeper and Other Poems,* by Langston Hughes. Copyright 1932 by Alfred A.
Knopf, Inc., and renewed 1960 by Langston Hughes. Reprinted by permission of the publisher. **Myra Cohn Livingston:**
"'For Purple Mountains' Majesty,'" from *The Malibu and Other Poems,* by Myra Cohn Livingston. Copyright © 1972 by Myra
Cohn Livingston. Reprinted by permission of Marian Reiner for the author. **David McCord:** "This Is My Rock," from *One at
a Time,* by David McCord. Copyright 1929 by David McCord. First appeared in *The Saturday Review.* Reprinted by permis-
sion of Little, Brown and Company. **Lilian Moore:** "Shells," from *I Thought I Heard the City,* by Lilian Moore. Copyright ©
1969 by Lilian Moore. "Until I Saw the Sea," from *I Feel the Same Way,* by Lilian Moore. Copyright © 1967 by Lilian Moore.
Both are reprinted by permission of Marian Reiner for the author. **Mary O'Neill:** "Sound of Water," from *What Is That
Sound?* Atheneum, 1966. Copyright © 1966 by Mary O'Neill. Reprinted by permission of International Creative Manage-
ment, Inc.

Library of Congress Cataloging-in-Publication Data

Land, sea, and sky : poems to celebrate the earth / selected and illustrated with
photographs by Catherine Paladino. — 1st ed.
    p. cm.
    Summary: A collection of poems celebrating nature, by such authors as Walt
Whitman, Langston Hughes, and Myra Cohn Livingston.
    ISBN 0-316-68892-4
    1. Nature — Juvenile poetry. 2. Nature — Pictorial works. 3. Children's poetry,
American. [1. Nature — Poetry. 2. American poetry — Collections.]
    I. Paladino, Catherine. II. Title.
    PS595.N22L36 1993
    811.008'036 — dc20   92-1284

Joy Street Books are published by Little, Brown and Company (Inc.)

10 9 8 7 6 5 4 3 2 1

SC

Published simultaneously in Canada
by Little, Brown & Company (Canada) Limited

Printed in Hong Kong

For three who made this journey with me:

Ann Rider, who led the way;

My dear husband, Scott, who carried my bags;

And my little son, Lukas, who came along for the ride

The earth hears you, the sky and timbered mountain see you. If you believe this, you will grow old. And you will see your sons and daughters and you will counsel them in this manner, when you reach your old age.

from "Counsel to Boys"
Luiseño

Contents

Looking Around

Bees
    own the clover,
birds
    own the sky,
rabbits,
    the meadow
    with low grass and high.

Frogs
    own the marshes,
ants
    own the ground . . .
    I hope they don't mind
    my looking around.

Aileen Fisher

"For Purple Mountains' Majesty"

I saw them today.
I saw them.
So many years I have heard them in a song.
It's true. They're purple when you see them.
They rise like kings.
They are mountains.
Suddenly
I know.
I *really* know
What that song is all about.

Myra Cohn Livingston

My great corn plants,
Among them I walk.
I speak to them;
They hold out their hands to me.

My great squash vines,
Among them I walk.
I speak to them;
They hold out their hands to me.

Navajo

This Is My Rock

This is my rock
And here I run
To steal the secret of the sun;

This is my rock
And here come I
Before the night has swept the sky;

This is my rock,
This is the place
I meet the evening face to face.

David McCord

The Little Rose Tree

Every rose on the little tree
Is making a different face at me!

Some look surprised when I pass by,
And others droop — but they are shy.

These two whose heads together press
Tell secrets I could never guess.

Some have their heads thrown back to sing,
And all the buds are listening.

I wonder if the gardener knows,
Or if he calls each just a rose?

Rachel Field

Trees

Trees are the kindest things I know,
They do no harm, they simply grow

And spread a shade for sleepy cows,
And gather birds among their boughs.

They give us fruit in leaves above,
And wood to make our houses of,

And leaves to burn on Hallowe'en,
And in the spring new buds of green.

They are the first when day's begun
To touch the beams of morning sun,

They are the last to hold the light
When evening changes into night,

And when a moon floats on the sky,
They hum a drowsy lullaby

Of sleepy children long ago . . .
Trees are the kindest things I know.

Harry Behn

The Wolf

When the pale moon hides and the wild wind wails,
And over the tree-tops the nighthawk sails,
The gray wolf sits on the world's far rim,
And howls: and it seems to comfort him.

The wolf is a lonely soul, you see,
No beast in the wood, nor bird in the tree,
But shuns his path; in the windy gloom
They give him plenty, and plenty of room.

So he sits with his long, lean face to the sky
Watching the ragged clouds go by.
There in the night, alone, apart,
Singing the song of his lone, wild heart.

Far away, on the world's dark rim
He howls, and it seems to comfort him.

Georgia Roberts Durston

Feather or Fur

When you watch for
Feather or fur
Feather or fur
Do not stir
Do not stir.

Feather or fur
Come crawling
Creeping
Some come peeping
Some by night
And some by day.
Most come gently
All come softly
Do not scare
A friend away.

When you watch for
Feather or fur
Feather or fur
Do not stir
Do not stir.

John Becker

Until I Saw the Sea

Until I saw the sea
I did not know
that wind
could wrinkle water so.

I never knew
that sun
could splinter a whole sea of blue.

Nor
did I know before,
a sea breathes in and out
upon a shore.

Lilian Moore

Shells

The bones of the sea
are on the shore,
shells
curled into the sand,
shells
caught in green weed hair.
All day I gather them
and there are always
more.

I take them home,
magic bones of the sea,
and when
I touch one,
then I hear
I taste
I smell the sea
again.

Lilian Moore

Sound of Water

The sound of water is:
Rain,
Lap,
Fold,
Slap,
Gurgle,
Splash,
Churn,
Crash,
Murmur,
Pour,
Ripple,
Roar,
Plunge,
Drip,
Spout,
Skip,
Sprinkle,
Flow,
Ice,
Snow.

Mary O'Neill

Whale

A whale is stout about the middle,
He is stout about the ends,
& so is all his family
& so are all his friends.

He's pleased that he's enormous,
He's happy he weighs tons,
& so are all his daughters
& so are all his sons.

He eats when he is hungry
Each kind of food he wants,
& so do all his uncles
& so do all his aunts.

He doesn't mind his blubber,
He doesn't mind his creases,
& neither do his nephews
& neither do his nieces.

You may find him chubby,
You may find him fat,
But he would disagree with you:
He likes himself like that.

Mary Ann Hoberman

How to Tell the Top of a Hill

The top of a hill
Is not until
The bottom is below.
And you have to stop
When you reach the top
For there's no more UP to go.

To make it plain
Let me explain:
The one *most* reason why
You have to stop
When you reach the top — is:
The next step up is sky.

John Ciardi

'll tell you how the sun rose, —
A ribbon at a time.
The steeples swam in amethyst,
The news like squirrels ran.

The hills untied their bonnets,
The bobolinks begun.
Then I said softly to myself,
"That must have been the sun!"

Emily Dickinson

Snowstorm

The sky
kept falling, falling,
in fluffy bits of white.

The sky
kept spilling over
everywhere in sight.

I never knew
it was so big,
it fell all day and night.

Aileen Fisher

April Rain Song

Let the rain kiss you.

Let the rain beat upon your head with silver liquid drops.

Let the rain sing you a lullaby.

The rain makes still pools on the sidewalk.

The rain makes running pools in the gutter.

The rain plays a little sleep-song on our roof at night —

And I love the rain.

Langston Hughes

28

I See the Moon

I see the moon,
And the moon sees me;
God bless the moon,
And God bless me.

Anonymous

The poem is arranged in two voices side by side, to be read aloud together.

Voice 1	Voice 2
We were counted not in	
	thousands
nor	
	millions
but in	
billions.	*billions.*
	We were numerous as the
stars	stars
	in the heavens
As grains of	
sand	sand
at the sea	
	As the
buffalo	buffalo
	on the plains.
When we burst into flight	
	we so filled the sky
that the	
sun	sun
was darkened	
	and
day	day
	became dusk.
Humblers of the sun	Humblers of the sun
we were!	we were!
The world	
inconceivable	inconceivable
	without us.
Yet it's 1914,	
and here I am	
alone	alone
	caged in the Cincinnati Zoo.
the last	
	of the passenger pigeons.

The Passenger Pigeon
To be read in two voices

Paul Fleischman

Who Am I?

The trees ask me,
And the sky,
And the sea asks me
Who am I?

The grass asks me,
And the sand,
And the rocks ask me
Who I am.

The wind tells me
At nightfall,
And the rain tells me
Someone small.

Someone small
Someone small
But a piece
of
it
all.

Felice Holman